# JEFFERSON'S BOOKS

# JEFFERSON'S BOOKS

*Douglas L. Wilson*

Preface by Daniel J. Boorstin

THOMAS JEFFERSON MEMORIAL FOUNDATION

*Monticello Monograph Series*

*1996*

# THE THOMAS JEFFERSON MEMORIAL FOUNDATION, INC.

This publication was made possible by a gift from Luella and Martin Davis.

Originally printed as "Jefferson's Library." Reprinted with permission of Charles Scribner's Sons, an imprint of Simon & Schuster Macmillan, from THOMAS JEFFERSON: A REFERENCE BIOGRAPHY, Merrill D. Peterson, Editor. Copyright © 1986 Charles Scribner's Sons.

Preface copyright © 1995 by Daniel J. Boorstin
Inset cover photograph © 1996 by R Lautman/Thomas Jefferson Memorial Foundation, Inc. All rights reserved.

Designed by Gibson Parsons Design.
Printed by Progress Printing, Lynchburg, Virginia.

ISBN 1-882886-03-8

# PREFACE

To catch Jefferson's spirit, we should write not of Jefferson's library, but of Jefferson's libraries. As Douglas L. Wilson recounts in this excellent essay, they were always growing and widening and deepening—collections being restlessly built and rebuilt. Not only did books inform and guide Jefferson's life in a way with no precedent and few equals among American statesmen. The building of libraries concentrated Jefferson's intellectual energies again and again. When his first personal library of some 300-400 books was burned at Shadwell in 1770 in the fire that destroyed the house in which he had been born, he calculated its loss at £200 and lamented, "Would to god it had been the money; then had it never cost me a sigh!" By the time Jefferson arrived in Paris in 1784 for his commercial and diplomatic mission, his new personal library, by his own count, had already numbered some 2,640 volumes.

During his five years in Paris, Wilson reminds us, he frequented "all the principal bookstores, turning over every book with my own hand, and putting by everything which related to America, and indeed whatever was rare and valuable in every science." On his return home, he had added at least 2,000 volumes, and he never ceased collecting. Then when the British burned the congressional library in the capitol in 1814, as Wilson explains, Jefferson seized the opportunity to renew the nation's library. He offered his library (which he estimated at "seven or eight thousand volumes") on condition that it be accepted in its entirety. "I envy you that immortal honor," was the dour John Adam's comment on hearing that Jefferson's offer had been accepted. Jefferson now asked for the privilege of retaining "a few of the books, to amuse the time I have yet to pass." But he actually did not retain any. Now again, Jefferson proved, as he said, "I cannot live without books," when he collected a wholly new retirement library. This was a collection for "amusement and not use" focused on subjects of his deepest and most personal interest. This library itself had few equals among personal libraries in the country at the time. It included essays, poetry, classics, and politics, along with *Don Quixote*, said to be the only novel he ever reread. He continued to collect and had finally acquired some 1,600 volumes.

As Jefferson's last library revealed, books were for him not ornaments but instruments for coming to terms with the world. His three idols were Francis Bacon, John Locke, and Isaac Newton. He based his classification scheme (from Bacon's *Advancement of Learning*) on the faculties of Memory, Reason and Imagination. Always ready to provide reading lists for young friends, he even obliged them by classifying books by the time of day when they should best be read, because "a great inequality is observable to the vigor of the mind at different periods of the day." Which put Belles-Lettres last—for the hours from dark until bedtime. In times of political crisis, when others might have been preoccupied by current events, Jefferson dug still deeper into history. And his *Summary View of the Rights of British America* (1774) which first brought him wide public notice, though a political tract, was founded on his knowledge of the earliest period of British history.

Practical interests appeared not only in Jefferson's books on botany, biology, agriculture, landscaping and architecture, but in subtler ways. Instead of the common alphabetical arrangement of titles he preferred arrangement by subject-matter. And for quite practical reasons. He had found the alphabetical arrangement "very unsatisfactory, because of the medley it presents to the mind, the difficulty sometimes of recalling an author's name, and the greater difficulty ... of selecting the word in the title, which shall determine its alphabetical place." He also preferred chronological and analytical arrangements of titles. While other cataloguers had commonly given a conspicuous place to theology, he offended some of the pious by treating religion as part of jurisprudence (leaving out theology) because it provided the institutions for enforcing morality.

Jefferson's passion for books, as Wilson notes, remained the solace for his life. "I have given up newspapers," he professed in 1812, "in exchange for Tacitus and Thucydides, for Newton and Euclid; and I find myself much the happier." His lively intellectual companionship with John Adams in his last years proved to be an argumentative triangle, with books usually the other term. In a familiar, but rare, self-deprecation, Jefferson referred to his "quixotism for the diffusion of knowledge." But succeeding centuries would prove that there was good common sense in his defense of the breadth of his collection against know-nothing objections of Federalists like Cyrus King who opposed the national purchase of his library because it would only spread his "infidel philosophy" with books "good, bad , and indifferent, old, new, and worthless, in languages which many cannot read and most ought not."

The following century would amply justify Jefferson's prediction that "there is, in fact, no subject to which a member of Congress may not have occasion to refer." He foresaw a great cosmopolitan library as the indispensable instrument of enlight-ened representative government. And the Congress affirmed his legacy in 1980 when it christened the first and grandest Library of Congress building by the name of Thomas Jefferson.

— DANIEL J. BOORSTIN

*A view of Jefferson's book room at Monticello, looking East from his study, or "cabinet." In Jefferson's day, this suite of rooms at the South end of the first floor would have been filled to overflowing with books.*

When news reached Thomas Jefferson in September 1814 that the invading British army had burned the Capitol building in Washington and destroyed the congressional library, he made a momentous decision. He sat down and wrote a letter offering Congress his own collection of books and manuscripts as a replacement, making one condition—that his library must be accepted in its entirety. If Congress were agreeable to this, he would accept whatever compensation its members thought fit to provide. The former president could not have foreseen all the implications of this fateful decision, but he was certainly aware of some of them. He knew that the congressional collection was much smaller and more narrowly based than his own, for he had materially contributed to its development during his term as president. He knew, therefore, that acceptance of his library would constitute a considerable upgrading of the congressional collection. And he knew enough about congressmen to expect that eyebrows would be raised at any "unnecessary" expenditures, such as those for books not dealing with law and government. Anticipating this objection, he wrote of his library to Samuel H. Smith on 21 September 1814: "I do not know that it contains any branch of science which Congress would wish to exclude from their collection; there is, in fact, no subject to which a member of Congress may not have occasion to refer."[1] He must also have had some idea that the library would ultimately reach a larger public than members of Congress and the government. What he may not have foreseen, but what would have given him the greatest satisfaction, was that his collection would become the foundation of a great national library, and that its acquisition and special character would prove the inspiration for a Library of Congress that would embrace the whole expanse of human knowledge and be open and free to all.

Jefferson's letter to Smith, a Washington newspaper editor and close friend who was to be his agent in the negotiations that followed, included for the inspection of the joint library committee a handwritten catalog of his library, which he had made in 1812. In this letter he characterized his collection, described the care with which it had been chosen, and made the case for its fitness as a replacement for the lost congressional library. He pointed first to its richness in "works relating to America," many of which he had acquired while living in Europe:

> ... in that department particularly, such a collection was made as probably can never again be effected, because it is hardly probable that the same opportunities, the same time, industry, perseverance and expense, with some knowledge of the bibliography of the subject would again happen to be in concurrence. During the same period, and after my return to America, I was led to procure, also, whatever related to the duties of those in the high concerns of the nation. So that the collection, which I suppose is of between nine and ten thousand volumes, while it includes what is chiefly valuable in science and literature generally, extends more particularly to whatever belongs to the American statesman.[2]

The congressional committee professed great interest but wanted to know how much the books were worth. Jefferson was unwilling to put a value on them himself and asked a Georgetown bookseller, Joseph Milligan, who was familiar with his library, to make an exact count from the catalog and suggest an average price per volume. Milligan's count was 6,487 volumes, far short of Jefferson' estimate, and less even than an earlier estimate Jefferson had made of "seven or eight thousand volumes." He had expressed to Smith the hope that Congress would allow him "to retain a few of the books, to amuse the time I have yet to pass," which would revert to Congress on his death. "Those I should like to retain would be chiefly classical and mathematical. Some few in other branches, and particularly one of the five encyclopedias in the catalogue. But this, if not acceptable, would not be urged." Unfortunately for Jefferson, the question was never put, and Milligan's formula—"for a folio ten dollars, for a quarto six dollars, for an octavo three dollars, for a duodecimo one dollar"—when approved by Jefferson, was translated into a total price of $23,950 and promptly written into the committee's resolution.[3]

With the price thus fixed for the Monticello library and with no express provision for his retaining any books for his personal use, Jefferson began to fear that the number of books listed in the catalog but missing from the library might be large and the books themselves difficult to replace. "The compensation embracing the whole of the catalogue, I shall not retain a single one," he wrote Smith on 27 February 1815, "the only modification to be made being a deduction from the compensation in proportion to the size and number of the books which on review shall appear to have been lost." Upon the return of the catalog in March 1815, Jefferson made his own count, carefully comparing the catalog to the volumes on his shelves, and arrived at a grand total of 6,707. Greatly relieved to discover that the volumes not entered exceeded those that were missing, he duly included them in the catalog and the library, remarking pointedly to the secretary of the treasury, Alexander J. Dallas, when he applied for payment in 18 April 1815: "I have not thought it right to withdraw these from the library, so that the whole delivered exceeds on the principles of the estimate, the sum appropriated."[4]

Meanwhile the congressional deliberations, once they reached the floor of the House of Representatives, were far from disinterested and had become blatantly partisan. The political opponents of Jefferson and his party made the most of the fact that the country was at war and in debt and that many of the books in Jefferson's library seemed outside the purview of a congressional library. The most outspoken Federalist opponent, Cyrus King, argued that Jefferson's books would help disseminate his "infidel philosophy" and were "good, bad, and indifferent, old, new, and worthless, in languages which many can not read, and most ought not." In the end, the purchase was agreed to by a narrow margin along party lines, but the spirit of the opposition is captured in the grudging comment of the *Boston Gazette*: "The grand library of Mr. Jefferson will undoubtedly be purchased with all its finery and philosophical nonsense."[5]

When these matters were decided, Jefferson began calculating the volume and weight of the books and determining the best method of packing and shipping them to Washington. That he took the trouble to find out how many wagons would be needed, what it would cost to hire them, and what would be the best route for the wagon train to take was characteristic of the man and his meticulous concern for detail. After the catalog had been carefully revised, labels were pasted on the spine of

This shows one side of the tally sheet created by Jefferson in 1815 to verify, chapter by chapter, the number of books in his library. By reference to his catalogue, he was also able to list those that were missing.

each book, giving the number of the section or "chapter" to which it belonged and its order within the chapter. Like most libraries of his day, Jefferson's was shelved by format or size, with the duodecimos and petit format volumes occupying the upper shelves, octavos and quartos the middle and somewhat deeper shelves, and the folios ranked at the bottom. In shipping his books, Jefferson first protected them with waste paper and then nailed boards across the front of the presses, so that they functioned as shipping crates in transit and permanent bookcases when set up in Blodget's Hotel, the temporary Capitol. By the middle of April ten wagons were loaded and on their way to Washington, carrying in them the foundation of an altogether new and revolutionary Library of Congress.

### THE BEGINNINGS OF THE LIBRARY

Peter Jefferson, the father of the future president, was without formal education but according to his son "read much and improved himself." By the time Thomas was sent to school at the age of five he was said to have read all the books in his father's modest library. At nine he was placed in the Latin school of the Reverend William Douglas, where he encountered a more substantial library and where he seems to have begun a collection of his own, for his father's account book records the expenditure of a sizable sum, £1/10/6 for "Books for my Son." At the death of Peter Jefferson in 1757, the 14-year-old Thomas inherited some forty-odd volumes, which must be regarded as the core of his first collection. This was a conventional planter's library, consisting mainly of practical and nondescript items, but it also contained Rapin's *History of England*, Anson's *Voyages*, and such literary favorites as the works of Addison and *The Spectator*.[6]

In 1758 he was sent to a more accomplished schoolmaster, the Reverend James Maury, to acquire, in accordance with the dying wishes of his father, a classical education. There he met with a library of at least two or three hundred volumes, as well as a learned and discriminating advisor, whom he described in his autobiography as "a correct classical scholar." Maury's advice to his son may have been urged on his other pupils as well, for its message was very much taken to heart by the young Jefferson:

I would recommend it to you to reflect, and remark on, and digest what you read; to enter into the spirit and design of your author; to observe every step he takes to accomplish his end; and to dwell on any remarkable beauties of diction, justness or sublimity of sentiment, or masterly strokes of true wit which may occur in the course of your reading.

Jefferson was by every account an unusually apt and studious pupil, and it was probably during his two years at Maury's school that he began to keep a commonplace book of his reading, the better to fix in his mind the beauties and retain the masterly strokes. In his commonplace book he began first with the classical writers—Horace, Cicero, Ovid, and Virgil—and then went on to make extracts from the great English poets— Pope, Milton, and Shakespeare. During these years he was a "hard student," and years later he was recalled as being habitually seen with a book in his hand—a Greek grammar.[7]

When he entered the College of William and Mary in 1760, Jefferson at last had access to an institutional library and found himself for the first time within reach of a shop where he could buy books. He lived in Williamsburg on a regular basis for two years as a college student and intermittently for five years thereafter as a student of the law under the tutelage of George Wythe. A sample of his Williamsburg book purchases survives in the daybooks of the *Virginia Gazette*, the leading bookstore in the colony. From these we learn that during the years 1764 and 1765, he bought 32 titles, amounting to 56 volumes. Predictably, the largest category (nine books) is law. Next largest (five books) is history; "when young I was passionately fond of reading history," Jefferson later reported. The *Virginia Gazette* purchases included Enrico Caterino Davila's history of the civil war in France, David Hume's *History of England*, William Robertson's *History of Scotland*, and William Stith's *History of the First Discovery and Settlement of Virginia*. Three works in Italian, plus an Italian-English dictionary, testify that he was teaching himself in 1764 to read that language,which, along with French and Spanish, was one of three modern languages he eventually mastered. The other notable category is poetry, including the works of John Milton, Edward Young, and William Shenstone, all of which he read and extracted in his commonplace and memorandum books. Classical litera-ture, agriculture, medicine, and religion were also represented by one or two titles, affirming the fact that the remarkable breadth of interests he exhibited in later life was an early phenomenon. In light of their subsequent importance in Jefferson's de-velopment, the presence of two other volumes should be noted: an influential work on landscape gardening, which he referred to as *James on Gardening*, and a vol-ume designated *Bacon's Philosophy*. Landscape gardening became one of his most ab-sorbing artistic interests, an art that he never failed to study in his travels and to practice at Monticello all his life. Bacon he came to regard, with Locke and New-ton, as one the three greatest men that ever lived.[8]

Invaluable as the daybooks are, they reveal nothing of the books that Jefferson must have been acquiring from abroad. The books imported for resale by the *Vir-ginia Gazette* were very expensive, and the selection was limited. The literary and le-gal commonplace books that Jefferson was keeping during these years help to fill in our picture of his reading and, in all likelihood, his library. He was fond of English poetry, and, in addition to the writers already mentioned, he read and common-placed the Scottish poet, James Thomson, whose glorification of rural life and landscape in the manner of Virgil's *Georgics* attracted him, and another popular eighteenth-century poet, Mark Akenside. We know that he liked to see plays, and the Literary Commonplace Book shows that he read them as well. He was also reading and commonplacing at great length two writers who had a profound affect on his developing sensibility and modes of thought: the English politician and phi-losopher, Lord Bolingbroke, and the Scottish jurist, Lord Kames. Passages copied from Bolingbroke's deistic arguments in his *Philosophical Works* fill more pages in the Literary Commonplace Book than any other work, just as Kames's *Principles of Eq-uity* predominates in his Equity Commonplace Book. Jefferson's rationalistic deism and his deeply rooted belief in natural rights, both of which contributed signifi-cantly to the character of his thought, owed much to the reading of these two works in the mid-1760s. He seems to have read and been influenced by other books by Lord Kames during this period, most notably a key work on aesthetics, *Elements of Criticism*, and *Essays on the Principles of Morality and Natural Religion*. Kames, who was represented in Jefferson's mature library by no fewer than 10 titles, was himself a famous lawyer and legal scholar with universal interests and must be regarded as one of Jefferson's early role models.

One further glimpse of his first library comes by way of an invoice of books purchased from London in 1769. This was the year that Jefferson was first elected to public office, and the 13 books listed all reflect an interest in legislation and government. Half of the books are on the history and workings of Parliament, a subject that Jefferson was to research with great care; but even more important for the momentous turn that his mind was about to take were a half-dozen works of political theory, including treatises by Montesquieu, Burlamaqui, and Locke. The young lawyer, whose knowledge and range of interests had constantly been expanded through reading and study, now applied himself in the same way to the questions of politics, though he often complained in later life that the need to study politics had taken him away from intellectual pursuits that were more congenial to his scholarly temperament.[9]

## A MORE EXTENSIVE PLAN

On 1 February 1770, a fire destroyed the house he had been born in at Shadwell, and most of Thomas Jefferson's library was lost. A family tradition has it that his first reaction on learning of the fire, which happened while he was away, was to inquire after the fate of his books. There is no doubt that he would have regarded his library as his most valuable possession, and not merely for the cash value it represented. On 20 February, he wrote to his college friend, John Page: "My late loss may perhaps have reached you by this time, I mean the loss of my mother's house by fire, and in it, of every paper I had in the world, and almost every book. On a reasonable estimate I calculate the cost of the books burned to have been £200. sterling. Would to god it had been the money; then had it never cost me a sigh!"[10]

Jefferson had been a serious collector of books for about 10 years, and during that time he was first a student, and then a practitioner of the law. "Nothing is more remarkable about his youth," Merrill D. Peterson has written, "than his love of books and learning." The library at Shadwell probably contained the standard works found in most Virginia collections of the time: *The Spectator*, *Paradise Lost*, the Bible, the *Book of Common Prayer*, Shakespeare's plays, Pope's works, *The Tatler*, Richard Allestree's *The Whole Duty of Man*, the laws of Virginia, Dryden's Virgil, and Butler's *Hudibras*. But Jefferson was not an ordinary reader nor did his library long remain conventional. It seems likely from their early bookmarks, for example, that two standard reference works on the ancient world were there: John Potter's *Antiquities of Greece* and Basil Kennett's *Antiquities of Rome*. In addition to legal works, which may have predominated, the library must have contained books on the subjects in which he had a demonstrated interest: history, classics, philosophy, English poetry, languages, architecture, mathematics, music, natural science, and, most recently, politics. The most tangible clue to its size is the £200 "reasonable estimate" Jefferson made of its value, but this is by no means a precise indicator. A comparison of the prices paid for the books purchased in Williamsburg from the *Virginia Gazette* with those he would cite a few years later suggests that Williamsburg prices were much higher than those imported directly from London, and that law books, of which he apparently had many, were more expensive than most others. Considering these factors, we may estimate the library lost in the Shadwell fire at 300-400 volumes.[11]

For his time and place, particularly for a young man of 26, this was a huge library. Even for a rich man, which Jefferson was, it represented a tremendous financial investment, being worth as much as a day laborer might expect to earn in 10 years, or equal to the cost of a herd of nearly 200 cows. But large and valuable as his first library undoubtedly was, Jefferson's ideas for a replacement were far more ambitious. To some extent, the Shadwell library had been a circumstantial accumulation, beginning with the inheritance of his father's books and gaining additions with each successive intellectual venture—studying law, learning Italian and Anglo-Saxon, designing Monticello, serving in the legislature. Now he was free to indulge his wide-ranging intellectual interests and his passion for books in a grand plan for a library that would embrace virtually all of human knowledge. He may well have had such a plan in mind earlier, but the Shadwell fire forced the issue and offered a rare opportunity to give his plan the name of action.[12]

Jefferson's grand plan for his library almost certainly had a model. While he had only made one foray outside of Virginia and had had little opportunity to observe large collections, he had undoubtedly seen the great library of William Byrd II of Westover, which was one of the marvels of the American colonies. William Byrd II (who died a year after Jefferson's birth) had been a wealthy Virginia landowner, who was educated in England and made a member of the Royal Society at age 22. He had assembled a collection of books on his Virginia plantation that was so large as to be awesome by contemporary standards. Arranged, cataloged, and cared for by a resident librarian, it numbered an unprecedented 3,500 volumes. But perhaps of more importance for the omnivorous young Jefferson was its unusually broad range. The Greek and Roman classics formed one of the most imposing parts of the library, while substantial sections were given over to typical categories such as law, divinity, and medicine. But quite untypically, one of the largest sections was classified as "Entertainment, Poetry, Translations, &c." where, according to Louis B. Wright, "the works of the Elizabethan and Restoration dramatists were more completely represented than in any other American library." It contained

> a large number of books of architecture, including the works of Vitruvius, Palladio, and more recent writers on that subject; a sizable collection of books on drawing and painting; collections of music, including examples of Italian and English operas; many books of philosophy, classical and modern—among them the works of Hobbes, Descartes, Boyle, Shaftesbury, Locke, and other relatively recent writers; twenty or more works on gardening and agriculture; an ample assortment of other utilitarian books, such as treatises on distilling, cookery, and related subjects; a scattering of textbooks on language, rhetoric, mathematics, and logic ….
>
> [Moreover, it represented] a carefully balanced collection of the best literature and learning of the day [that] had no equal in America.[13]

Whether he was closely familiar with the Westover library or knew it mostly by reputation, its grand scale and universal scope must have made a lasting impression on the young Jefferson, who was already gaining a reputation as one of the most precocious young men in the colony. Three years after the fire he seems to have visited Westover to consider the possibility of buying the great library for himself, for he listed in his 1773 Memorandum Book, under the heading "Westover library," the numbers of volumes by format (that is, folio, quarto, octavo, and so on) and price, calculating the size of the library at 3,486 volumes and the total price at £1219/18. On the next page he seems to have calculated what he could realize from the sale of books in his own library that presumably could be spared, but he could only come up with 669 volumes with a total value of £218. Though his marriage the year before had doubled his considerable fortune, the difference of £1,000 was an astronomical sum and must have far exceeded his means. Eventually, the great library of William Bryd II would find a buyer in Isaac Zane, who in 1778 purchased the entire collection and carried it to Philadelphia for resale. In the years that followed, having missed a unique opportunity to accomplish a major portion of his grand plan at a single stroke, Jefferson nonetheless acquired a good many Westover volumes for his own library.[14]

An important indication of Jefferson's grand plan for his library is contained in a remarkable letter he wrote on 3 August 1771 to Robert Skipwith, who had requested a list of books "suited to the capacity of a common reader who understands but little of the classicks and who has not leisure for any intricate or tedious study," costing £25 or £30. Jefferson's reply and the accompanying list of 148 titles are revealing documents, but due notice must be taken of Skipwith's phrasing, which is pointedly intended to underscore the difference between his own conventional interests and those of his scholarly advisor. While there is no doubt that the list, which lists prices and the address of a London bookseller, is an outgrowth of Jefferson's energetic efforts to rebuild his library after the 1770 fire and that it contains many books that were personal favorites and influential in his development, it is not modeled after his own library. This is most evident in its range and proportions. For example, nearly half of the items on the list are the works of English literary writers, a fair number of which—such as the novels of Henry Fielding, Samuel Richardson, and Tobias Smollett—Jefferson failed to acquire for himself, while only a small handful of books appear on subjects such as politics, natural science, and law, which bulked so large in Jefferson's own interests and in the collection he sold to Congress. Clearly he was attempting to heed Skipwith's admonitions and recommend something like a gentleman's library, but what he found himself unable to heed, significantly, was the limitation on cost, finally recommending a collection priced at more than £100. The letter to Skipwith that accompanies the list contains a defense of fiction that is often quoted, but Jefferson himself seems to have been little attracted to novels after his youth. The defense derives directly from Jefferson's reading of one of the books recommended, Lord Kames' *Elements of Criticism,* and Julian P. Boyd is probably right in observing that this defense is "less noteworthy ... than the up-to-the-minute character of the list," some of whose titles had been very recently published. Perhaps the most indicative thing in the letter in terms of his own library is his remark that Skipwith is welcome to come to Monticello, "from which you may reach your hand to a library formed on a more extensive plan."[15]

## BUILDING THE COLLECTION

The fire of 1770 gave new impetus both to the development of Jefferson's library and to his plans and efforts to build his own private residence, which he was then calling the Hermitage. The plan for the library seems to have been integral to the ambitious design of the whole. "It is clear," W. H. Adams writes, "from the earliest notes on Monticello that Jefferson intended its basic program to encompass the functions of a museum of art and of natural history as well as to house a comprehensive library ...." As he pushed his efforts to complete a livable portion of his new house, he moved just as vigorously to rebuild and expand his library. On 4 August 1773, according to his Memorandum Book, he counted the astonishing total of 1,256 volumes at Monticello, and these, he noted, did not include "vols. of Music; nor my books in Williams burgh." Thus, in three and a half years—during which he was managing a large estate, laboring under a heavy case load as a lawyer, courting and marrying a young widow, and building a new residence—he had managed to acquire a library collection three or four times as large as the one he had lost, averaging about one new book per day.[16]

While he must have succeeded in importing a substantial number of books from abroad, we know that he bought a great many books in America during these and succeeding years. The Westover library of William Byrd II eluded him, but he was more fortunate a few years later in acquiring what were probably two of the best libraries in Virginia, those of the illustrious Peyton Randolph and the learned Richard Bland. Randolph had inherited a valuable library from his father, Sir John Randolph, and Jefferson bought the entire collection, "book-cases and all as they stood." Richard Bland enjoyed a reputation as a "fine classical scholar" and a man whose "great learning lay in the field of British history in its largest sense, and especially that of Virginia." Both of these libraries contained manuscript records of early Virginia history, which Jefferson prized and carefully preserved, fully aware of their uniqueness and their historical importance.[17]

Years later, when the frontier had receded, Jefferson remarked "the difficulties of getting new works in our situation, inland and without a single bookstore." During the 1770s those difficulties were many times greater, for the problems of geography were compounded by the disruptions of war, domestic turmoil, and a wildly inflated currency. Still he succeeded by characteristic diligence in steadily adding to his book collection. When politics or his law practice took him to Williamsburg, he bought books at the office of the *Virginia Gazette*, which in 1775 listed some 300 titles available for sale. Books came to him at the deaths of his father-in-law, John Wayles, and his brother-in-law and closest friend, Dabney Carr. He purchased books from the estate of the Reverend James Horrocks, the president of the College of William and Mary, and from the collections of at least two members of the faculty, Reverend Samuel Henley and Thomas Gwatkin, who returned to England after the outbreak of hostilities in 1775. From Henley's varied collection he acquired an impressive array of books, including some standard authors—Dante, Milton, and Tasso—and some titles that were especially important to him, such as Thomas Whately's *Observations on Gardening* and the botanical works of Linnaeus. From the library of the fleeing Royal Governor of Virginia, Lord Dunmore, some books found their way into Jefferson's library, and from the estate of one Parson Wiley he acquired a run of early Viriginia newspapers that he believed to be unique.[18]

Being a member of the Continental Congress in 1775 and 1776 meant having access to the bookstores of Philadelphia, the commercial and cultural heart of the colonies, and his memorandum books attest that Jefferson made the most of his opportunity. With the ready availability of books, he recorded more purchases in his Memorandum Book for 1776 than in any previous year. His correspondence reveals that during the memorable session in which he produced the Declaration of Independence, his thoughts were often on his library. When word reached him of the availability of Gwatkin's books, he wrote at once for a catalog and asked his friend John Page to purchase immediately "two of them which I recollect he had and have long wished to get." He was greatly concerned about the fate of the books he had left in Williamsburg, which was in danger of becoming enemy territory, and sent directions for their removal. Later, as governor of Virginia, he was to do the same for his Monticello books when the British threatened Charlottesville in 1781.[19] When he decided to accept a diplomatic appointment in France in 1782, one of the attractions of Europe was the opportunity to further enhance his library. Waiting to take ship in Philadelphia, he roomed with his friend, James Madison, who was preparing a list of books to be included in a library that he hoped to persuade the Congress to establish, and the two men apparently exchanged bibliographies and desiderata lists. Jefferson had with him a catalog of the books he owned and was including in it books he intended to purchase abroad. It was presumably the books he owned that he counted and recorded in the front of the catalog on 6 March 1783—2,640 volumes. If any further proof were needed that Jefferson had in mind a grand plan for his library, we have it here. Having painstakingly, over a period of 13 years, built a library that was one of the largest and finest in America, adding 200 volumes annually in the face of enormous difficulties, he embarked for Europe determined to make very substantial additions.[20]

In the letter offering his library to Congress in 1815, Jefferson described his Paris book collecting in some detail:

> While residing in Paris, I devoted every afternoon I was disengaged, for a summer or two, in examining all the principal bookstores, turning over every book with my own hand, and putting by everything which related to America, and indeed whatever was rare and valuable in every science. Besides this, I had standing orders during the whole time I was in Europe, on it's principal book-marts, particularly Amsterdam, Frankfort, Madrid and London, for such works relating to America as could not be found in Paris.

According to William H. Peden, the author of the most detailed study of the subject, Jefferson had not exaggerated, for the five years that he spent in Paris, 1784-1789, were "probably the most important ones during his entire career as a book collector." He regarded books as one of the few areas in which Europe had the advantage over his own country and therefore as her most valuable commodity for Americans. "In science, the mass of the people [of France] is two centuries behind ours; their literati half a dozen years before us. Books, really good, acquire just reputation in that time, and so become known to us and communicate to us all their advances in knowlege." In addition to frequenting the shops in Paris, where the offices of the honest bookseller Frouillé were particularly valued, Jefferson ordered heavily from the catalogs of London booksellers such as Lackington and John Stockdale, the man entrusted with the publication of *Notes on the State of Virginia*. Not content with these efforts, he used his friends and fellow diplomats as agents where he could not go in person, though the book-hunting chores he tirelessly performed for his friends back home far outnumbered his own requests for help. The books that he took particular pains to select for Madison played an important role in the latter's studious preparation for the constitutional convention. The amount of money that Jefferson spent for books while he was in Paris and throughout his life was prodigious, even for a wealthy Virginia planter. He was aware that his indulgence in books amounted to extravagance and sought to moderate it by buying cheaper and smaller format editions wherever possible, and driving a hard bargain when offered an expensive book. To one of his agents in London he wrote: "Sensible that I labour grievously under the malady of Bibliomanie, I submit to the rule of buying only at reasonable prices, as to a regimen necessary in that disease."[21]

Before he returned to America late in 1789, Jefferson compiled a separate catalog of the books he had purchased abroad. The majority of the books, not surprisingly, were in French, and the largest categories were Politics and Geography, with marked emphasis on books relating to America. Another notable concentration was in languages; grammars, dictionaries, and lexicons in both ancient and modern languages clearly had a high priority in his foreign purchases. Written in the tiny handwriting that he occasionally employed and arranged according to his own classification scheme, this undated catalog seems to contain books acquired for others as well as for himself, and the entries are such that an accurate title or volume count is difficult to arrive at. But it is safe to conclude that during his five years in Paris Jefferson managed to add at least 2,000 volumes to his library. This represents an increase of 75 percent over the 2,640 volumes he counted in March 1783 and probably does not include the books he acquired in Philadelphia, Annapolis, and elsewhere between that time and his departure for Europe in July 1784. Jefferson thus returned to America in the fall of 1789 the possessor of a magnificent library of approximately 5,000 volumes.[22]

Drawn almost immediately into Washington's cabinet upon his return and burdened for the next four years by the heavy demands of his office and political affairs, he seems not to have added greatly to his library. He had the Paris books with him in Philadelphia during much of this period, and he used them to good advantage in his work as Secretary of State, as shown by his well-known statement on relations with France, drawn up at the request of President Washington, in which he cites works he had acquired in Paris by Grotius, Wolf, Pufendorf, and Vattel. Before resigning his office at the end of 1793, he echoed sentiments he had uttered upon leaving his governorship in 1781, and would invoke again on leaving the presidency, on the pleasures of returning to his family, his farms, and his books. These were versions of a famous passage of Latin verse that had attracted his attention as a schoolboy, finding it in Horace and copying it into his Literary Commonplace Book: "O rural home: when shall I behold you! When shall I be able, now with books of the ancients, now with sleep and idle hours, to quaff sweet forgetfulness of life's cares." His library, from an early period, formed an essential part of his vision of the good life.[23]

Jefferson's retirement ended in 1797, when he took up his duties as Vice-President, and for the next twelve years, while serving in Philadelphia and Washington, he resumed the building up of his book collection with renewed vigor. Although he told a Paris bookseller in 1803 that "my collection of books is now so extensive, & myself so far advanced in life that I have little occasion to add to it," Peden has shown that he continued buying books from a host of booksellers. His many purchases during this period reflect a continued interest not only in reading but in the creation of a truly distinctive library, and it is clear that by this time his grand plan included creating a collection that was intended to have a utility well beyond what was required for his personal use. After assuming the presidency, he lent his considerable knowledge of bibliography and the book market to the task of assembling a congressional library, now rendered essential by the government's move from Philadelphia to the marshy shores of the Potomac. By this time, he was receiving regularly and in large numbers presentation copies of books from their authors, and in 1806 he was left the extensive library of his close friend and mentor, George Wythe, who allowed in his will that while his books were "perhaps not deserving a place in [Jefferson's] Museum," they were "the most valuable to him of any thing which I have power to bestow." There is little doubt that Wythe knew whereof he willed.[24]

While holding public office in New York, Philadelphia, and Washington, Jefferson assembled a reading library of standard authors and favorite books in smaller formats, many of which he had bought in Paris. Hampered since 1786 by a dislocated wrist, Jefferson found books in larger formats, such as folios and quartos, awkward to handle and came to prefer the smaller octavos and duodecimos, which had the added advantages of taking less space and being cheaper. On his retirement, he installed this select collection, which he called his "petit format library," at Poplar Forest, his plantation near Lynchburg, where he spent several weeks each year. Prominent in the petit format library, which in the end exceeded 650 volumes, were an edition of the English poets in 109 volumes and an edition of Shakespeare in 38, both published in London by John Bell. According to his biographer, Henry S. Randall, the petit format library at Poplar Forest contained "a considerable collection of Italian and French, and a few favorite Greek and Latin poets, and a larger number of prose writers of the same languages—all, it is unnecessary to say, in the original."[25]

## An Abundance of Books

The library in the first Monticello was a large room on the second floor directly above the parlor. When the house was rebuilt, this space was occupied by the dome room so much admired by Margaret Bayard Smith, and the books were moved to the suite of rooms at the south end of the first floor, which included his "cabinet," where he did much of his reading and writing. When Mrs. Smith visited Monticello in 1809, she was impressed by the strictness with which Jefferson's privacy in this suite was observed and called it his "sanctum sanctorum." Isaac Jefferson, a slave who spent much of his long life at Monticello, vividly recalled his master in his library:

> Old Master had abundance of books; sometimes would have twenty of 'em down on the floor at once—read fust one, then tother. Isaac has often wondered how Old Master came to have such a mighty head; read so many of them books; and when they go to him to ax him anything, he go right straight to the book and tell you all about it.

Isaac's recollections afford us a rare glimpse of Jefferson's characteristic way of using his library. That he liked to lay many books out on the floor so as to be able to consult and compare differing accounts underscores the utility, as opposed to the

*A view of Jefferson's "cabinet" or study at Monticello, where he did much of his reading and most of his writing. On his writing desk is his polygraph, a machine for making an exact copy of the document being written. His chair has candle holders at the end of either arm, for extra illumination. Next to the desk is his revolving bookstand.*

mere mania, of possessing a full range of books on subjects of interest. Moreover, Isaac's picture of his master going straight to a book when he was asked a question reinforces our sense, so apparent in other places, that Jefferson's prodigious and wide-ranging knowledge was largely drawn from his reading. "His library expressed much more than the instinct of a collector," his biographer, Merrill D. Peterson, has written. "Jefferson was dependent on books, tended to take his knowledge from them rather than from direct experience, and approached the world with studied eyes."[26]

One of the important aims of Jefferson's grand plan for his library was clearly to provide for the fullest possible access to information and ideas. The need to know seemed to come as naturally to him as the need to breathe. He spoke often of his belief that nature had formed him for study, and he exercised his remarkable powers of discipline to find time for reading even in the busiest and most hectic times of his life. His earliest interests were literary and philosophical, as his commonplace books attest, but the study of the law fed his interest in history, which in turn shaped his understanding of religious and political institutions. He acquired from his teacher at the College of William and Mary, Dr. William Small, a taste for mathematics, to which he returned in later life with relish. In his "Autobiography" he paid high tribute to Small, whose friendship and interest in his intellectual development, he declared, "probably fixed the destinies of my life." From Small he got his "first views of the expansion of science & of the system of things in which we are placed." His intense interest in this "system of things" never waned, and his library is a testament to his lifelong effort to come to terms with it.[27]

Jefferson also developed and used his library as a potential source of new knowledge, the sphere of research. As a young lawyer, perhaps inspired by the example of Lord Kames, he began collecting legal documents and court records. Kames had first made his mark as a legal scholar by assembling and publishing the important decisions and precedents of Scottish law, which had been neglected by the English reporters. Jefferson began in the early years of his legal career to perform the same task for Virginia and managed to salvage and preserve many documents that would otherwise have been lost. He assiduously collected information on the American Indians, particularly on their languages, in the belief that a sufficient mass of material and proper analysis would eventually provide answers to such questions as whether their ancestors had migrated from Asia. Unfortunately, his years of effort went for naught when this collection was stolen while being shipped back to Monticello from Washington. Besides being a collector of valuable research materials, Jefferson had preeminently the temperament and qualities of mind requisite for research, and he was doubtful that one could become learned by studying "mere compilers" rather than primary sources. For this reason, he lamented the preemptive use of Blackstone's *Commentaries* by law students and required those who studied with him to begin with more basic works, such as *Coke on Littleton.* "now men are born scholars, lawyers, Doctors," he commented wryly to John Tyler; "in our day this was confined to poets." He believed and tried by his practice to demonstrate that answers to important questions—philosophical, historical, political, or scientific— could very often be found or formed by determination and effort. A classic example of what resourcefulness and diligent research are capable of producing is his only book, *Notes on the State of Virginia* (1785), a carefully documented compilation of facts and interpretation. In it he strove to assemble a coherent and accurate account of his "country" from bits and pieces of information sought out by direct inquiry or found in widely scattered and often problematical sources. "A patient pursuit of facts, and cautious combination and comparison of them," he wrote in a footnote, "is the drudgery to which man is subjected by his Maker, if he wishes to attain sure knowledge."[28]

Thomas Jefferson's library was not only a locus for intellectual endeavor and research; it was also an active tool in the varied enterprises of its creator. Though its beginnings were shaped by the accidents of his father's death and his schooling, its first definite shape and character was that of a library to support the study and practice of law. When it was destroyed by fire in 1770, Jefferson complained to his friend Page: "To make the loss more sensible it fell principally on my books of common law, of which I have but one left, at that time lent out." The letter makes clear that he believed he couldn't practice law without books, though others, like his friend Patrick Henry, performed successfully at the bar with little or no recourse to them. As Edmund Randolph famously put it, "Mr. Jefferson drew copiously from the depths of the law, Mr. Henry from the recesses of the human heart."[29]

As the troubles between the colonies and Great Britain deepened in the early 1770s, Jefferson's readings in history and politics increased. By the time the law courts were closed in 1774, his political activities and researches had practically become a full-time occupation. In addition to his well-known role as a political leader and spokeman, his notebooks show that he seized upon the dispute with the mother country as the occasion for intense research into the history of Virginia, the prerogatives of Crown and Parliament, the nature of the English Constitution, the origin and development of the common law, the original basis of land tenure in Saxon England, and the makeup of various confederations of states. He went thoroughly into the literature of parliamentary procedure, an effort of scholarship that paid important dividends later, when he used his findings to compile the *Manual of Parliamentary Practice* adopted by the United States Senate. And when, during the Revolution, the government of Virginia was being reconstituted, he was a principal contributor to the revisal of its laws, a task for which his talents as a legal scholar and researcher were ideally suited and his library, indispensable.[30]

Even farming, to which he was born and bred, was something that Jefferson sought to master through books. To be sure, the age in which he lived had begun to take agriculture very seriously, and there were countless books produced on what were proclaimed modern and scientific methods. While he maintained his admiration for the writings of the ancients on the subject, he owned most of the agricultural books of his own time that were recognized as significant, and his letters show that he read them and weighed their merits. "I am much indebted to you," he wrote an English correspondent, "for Mr Kirwan's charming treatise on manures. Science never appears so beautiful as when applied to the uses of human life, nor any use of it so engaging as those of agriculture & domestic economy." For a man who used the words "beautiful" and "charming" sparingly, it is utterly indicative that he should employ them to describe science and a pamphlet on fertilizer.[31]

For a variety of reasons, none of which seems attributable to his characteristically studious approach to agriculture, Jefferson did not enjoy much success as a farmer. But he did succeed in spectacular fashion in another art he learned from books—architecture. Completely self-taught, Jefferson studied architecture to grasp and assimilate its principles and to enable himself to build in exemplary fashion. "It is not at all surprising," writes Dumas Malone, "that he turned to books .... His distinction lay in the fact that he referred to more books than others did, that he went beyond British works to more remote sources, that he attained results which accorded with his own superior tastes and special needs." The evidence that he consulted many books is found not only in his library, which has an extensive section devoted to the subject, but also on his architectural drawings themselves, where he has written references to the books containing his models and sources. His great master was the sixteenth-century Italian, Andrea Palladio, whose classic work, *The Four Books of Architecture*, set forth principles and practice based on an intensive study of Roman architecture and the exact proportions that they exhibited. Palladio was undoubtedly, like Lord Kames, another role model for the young Jefferson, and the opening of the Preface to his *Four Books* sounded a note that the student was often to echo: "it seemed to me a thing worthy of a man, who ought not to be born for himself only, but also for the utility of others, to publish the designs of those edifices, (in collecting which, I have employed so much time, and exposed myself to so many dangers)."[32]

Jefferson's library was constantly changing; what was true of his collection in 1815 may not have been true earlier. Nevertheless, the 6,700 volumes he sold to Congress represent the library in its most fully developed form. Perhaps the most striking thing about it is its amazing breadth. The major categories of knowledge are, as one would expect, abundantly represented, but the number and range of minor categories Jefferson included is extraordinary. Nowhere is this more readily apparent than in the section labeled Technical Arts. Here are subsections, to cite only a few, on Cooking, Brewing, Printing, Watchmaking, Writing, Dying, a substantial selection of works on Tactics, and two on Aeorstation, or flying. True to his claim, the library proves upon examination to be particularly well suited for "the American statesman." The section on Politics is immense, far and away the largest in the library and constituting more than a quarter of the entire collection. Its range extends from the great theoretical treatises of Aristotle, Plato, Machiavelli, Montesquieu, and Locke to the nameless hackwork of the ephemeral tract. To preserve the discourse of an age that carried on political disputation by exchanging printed salvos, Jefferson carefully organized and gathered into bound volumes hundreds of pamphlets. Quite

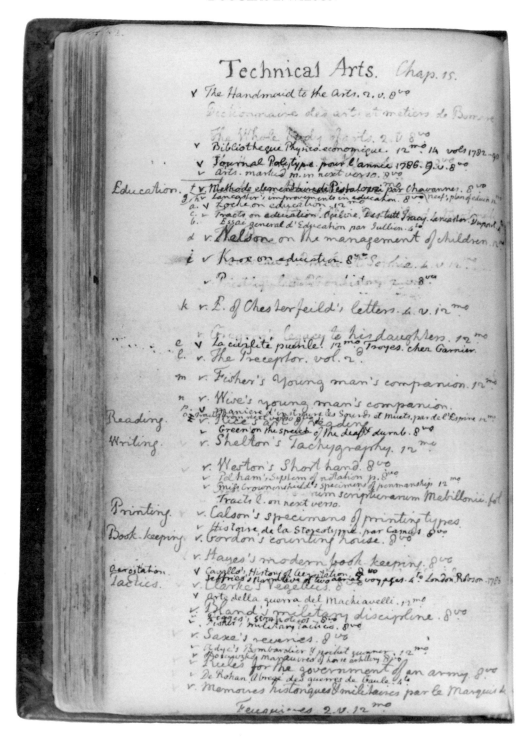

*A page from the "1783" manuscript catalog of Jefferson's library, showing the categories and entries listed under the chapter or section labeled "Technical Arts." Courtesy of the Massachusetts Historical Society.*

unobtrusively, in a surviving volume entered in the catalog as "Great Britain & America. tracts. 1765-1781. 10. v. 8ᵛᵒ," appears *A Summary View of the rights of British America*, a pamphlet written by Jefferson himself and published by his friends in 1774. The section on Politics is complemented by the next largest sections, Law and History. In both there is impressive historical range and depth, but the major preoccupation is with the legal and historical tradition to which Virginia and America belong. And in the sizable Geography section, the subject of America is predominant. More even than its size and remarkable range of subject matter, this extraordinary concentration of American material, as Peden has pointed out, is what is most distinctive about Jefferson's library. Congress may have lost a serviceable reference library to the British invaders, but it gained as a consequence an unparalleled collection of materials on its own country.

## CLASSIFICATION

Sometime before 1783, when he was preparing the list of books he wished to acquire in Europe, Jefferson began a classified catalog of his library. He had previously arranged books by categories in recommended reading lists, such as the Skipwith list of 1771. The books he recommended to Skipwith were grouped under nine headings:

Fine Arts

Criticism on the Fine Arts

Politicks, Trade

Religion

Law

History. Antient

History. Modern

Natural Philosophy, Natural History &c

Miscellaneous

In some of the numerous lists he compiled for law students, which were usually not confined to works on the law, he arranged the recommended categories of books by the time of the day at which they should be read, explaining to Bernard Moore: "a great inequality is observable in the vigor of the mind at different periods of the day. It's powers at these periods should therefore be attended to in marshal-ling the business of the day." Accordingly, he recommended the folowing reading schedule:

| Before eight: | Physical Studies, Ethics, Religion, Natural Law |
| Eight to twelve: | Law |
| Twelve to one: | Politics |
| In the afternoon: | History |
| From dark to bedtime: | Belles-lettres, Criticism, Rhetoric, Oratory[33] |

But when he came to catalog his library he chose a much more ambitious clas-sification scheme that aimed at encompassing all knowledge and was based on the faculties of the mind, a scheme set forth by Francis Bacon and promulgated in the eighteenth century by Jean Lerond D'Alembert in the first volume of the monu-mental *Encyclopédie*. Jefferson's version was his own adaptation, but he followed Ba-con and D'Alembert in embracing a correspondence between the faculties of Memory, Reason, and Imagination and the three principal categories of human knowledge: History, Philosophy, and Fine Arts. His basic classification scheme, more orderly and less vague than those of his models, reveals much about his own predispositions, as well the makeup of his library. As Arthur E. Bestor has written, Jefferson's classification scheme is "in some sense, a blueprint of his mind," but it also represents a practical accommodation to the kinds of books he had selected for himself. Jefferson speaks directly to this point in a letter of 7 May 1815 to the Librar-ian of Congress George Watterston:

> Thus the law having been my profession, and politics the occupation to which the circumstances of the times in which I have lived called my particular attention, my provision of books in these lines, and in those most nearly connected with them was more copious, and required in par-ticular instances subdivisions into sections and paragraphs, while other subjects of which general views only were contemplated are thrown into masses. A physician or theologist would have modified differently, the chapters, sections, and paragraphs of a library adapted to their particular pursuits.[34]

Books may be classed from the Faculties of the mind, which be

I. Memory.    II. Reason.    III. Imagination

are applied respectively to

I. History.    II. Philosophy.    III. Fine Arts.

| | | | | Chap. |
|---|---|---|---|---|
| | | Antient. | Antient hist. | 1. |
| | Civil proper. | | Foreign. | 2. |
| | | Modern. | British.. | 3. |
| Civil. | | | American. | 4. |
| | Ecclesiastical............. | | Ecclesiastical | 5. |
| | | | Nat.l Philos. | 6. |
| | | | Agriculture | 7. |
| History. | Physics............. | | Chemistry. | 8. |
| | | | Surgery. | 9. |
| | | | Medecine | 10. |
| | | Animals | Anatomy. | 11. |
| Natural. | | | Zoology. | 12. |
| | Nat.l hist.y prop. | Vegetables. | Botany. | 13. |
| | | Minerals. | Mineralogy | 14. |
| | Occupations of Man............. | | Technical arts. | 15. |

## CLASSIFICATION TABLE OF THE 1783 CATALOG

Books may be classed from the Faculties of the mind, which being
*I. Memory    II. Reason    III. Imagination*
are applied respectively to
*I. History    II. Philosophy    III. Fine Arts*

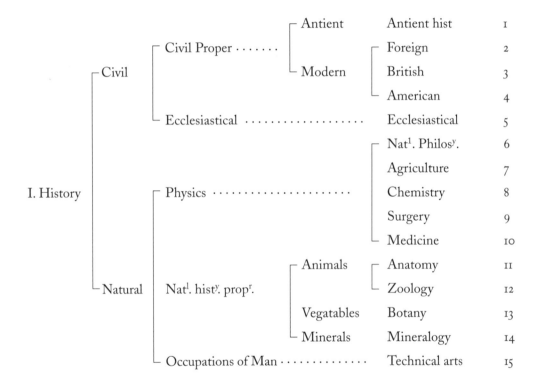

| | | | | |
|---|---|---|---|---|
| | | | Antient | Antient hist | 1 |
| | Civil Proper | Antient / Modern | Foreign | 2 |
| Civil | | | British | 3 |
| | | | American | 4 |
| | Ecclesiastical | | Ecclesiastical | 5 |

I. History

- Civil
  - Civil Proper
    - Antient — Antient hist — 1
    - Modern — Foreign — 2 / British — 3 / American — 4
  - Ecclesiastical — Ecclesiastical — 5
- Natural
  - Physics — Nat$^l$. Philos$^y$. — 6 / Agriculture — 7 / Chemistry — 8 / Surgery — 9 / Medicine — 10
  - Nat$^l$. hist$^y$. prop$^r$.
    - Animals — Anatomy — 11 / Zoology — 12
    - Vegatables — Botany — 13
    - Minerals — Mineralogy — 14
  - Occupations of Man — Technical arts — 15

11    Chap.

```
                                              * Moral Philos.
                        Ethics ..........................
                                                Law Nature & Nations    16.
                              Religious ..........  Religion.           17.
        Moral.
                                                    Equity.             18.
                                                    Common Law          19.
                                        Domestic.   L. Merchant.        20.
                        Jurisprudence               L. Maritime.        21.
                              Municipal.            L. Ecclesiast.      22.
                                        Foreign.    Foreign Law.        23.
                                                    Politics.           24.
                              Oeconomical. .........
Philosophy ..                                       Commerce.           25.

                                                    Arithmetic.         26.
                        Pure ..........................
                                                    Geometry            27.
                                                    Mechanics
                                                    St. Statics
        Mathematical                                Dynamics
                                                                        28.
                        Physico-Mathematical ............  Pneumatics
                                                    Phonics
                                                    Optics.
                                                    Astronomy.          29.
                                                    Geography.          30.
```

* in classing a small library one may throw under this
head books which attempt what may be called the Natural
history of the mind or an Analysis of it's operations. the term
and division of Metaphysics is rejected as meaning nothing
... something beyond our reach, or what should be called by
... other ...

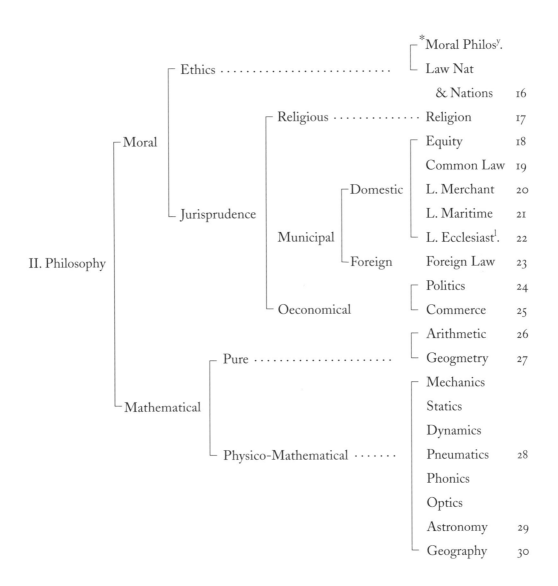

* in classing a small library one may throw under this head books
which attempt what may be called the Natural history of the mind
or an Analysis of it's operations. the term and division of
Metaphysics is rejected as meaning nothing or something beyond
our reach, or what should be called by another name.

| | | | | Chap. |
|---|---|---|---|---|
| | Gardening | | Gardening | 31. |
| | Architecture | | Architecture | 32. |
| | Sculpture | | Sculpture | 33. |
| | Painting | | Painting | 34. |
| | Music | Theoretical | Music. Theory | 35. |
| | | Practical | Music. Vocal | 36. |
| | | | Music. Instrument | 37. |
| | | Narrative | Epic | 38. |
| | | | Romance | 39. |
| III. Fine Arts. | Poetry | Dramatic | Tragedy | 40. |
| | | | Comedy | 41. |
| | | | Pastorals | |
| | | | Odes | 42. |
| | | | Elegies | |
| | | | Dialogue | |
| | | Didactic | Satire | |
| | | | Epigram | 43. |
| | | | Epistles | |
| | Oratory | | Logic | |
| | | | Rhetoric | 44. |
| | | | Oration | |
| | Criticism | | Criticism | 45. |
| Authors who have written in various branches | | | Polygraphical | 46. |

The 1783 manuscript catalog of his library shows evidence that the classification scheme employed there had undergone some evolution over the years, but the table he affixed to the front of the catalog represents the scheme in its most representive form.

Jefferson begins with the three basic divisions that he borrowed from Bacon and D'Alembert and then subdivides these as many as four times until he arrives at the numbered classes that he calls "chapters." The serious thought given to the ways in which different aspects of human knowledge interrelate is evident, but his principal aim is to arrive at meaningful classes for his books. A student of his various classifications schemes has noted that some of them, such as those found in his 1779 bill for the reorganization of the College of William and Mary or his 1818 plan for the University of Virginia, are so different from that of his library catalog "that they might well have been the products of different minds." One of the reasons for this is that Jefferson embarked upon the scheme with his own books and intellectual interests in mind. An obvious example is the classing under Civil History, which subdivides into Antient and Modern, with Modern being further broken down into Foreign, British, and American. Thus he begins with all of non-Ecclesiastical History and arrives at four classes or chapters perfectly adapted to his own interests. More idiosyncratic is his category for Foreign Law, which not only includes books on the law of foreign countries but on the law of the other American states as well. Books on the laws of Great Britain and Virginia appear in the chapter on Common Law, but those on Massachusetts, for example, are classed as foreign, apparently because of Jefferson's belief that the basis of law in the Eastern states was a "compound," put together from various sources, with "an abundance of notions of their own."[35]

The most conspicuous departure that Jefferson made from the schemes of his predecessors, as well as the most eye-catching innovation, was in his treatment of religion. Whereas Bacon and D'Alembert gave prominent places in their schemes to theology and the sacred, Jefferson's treating religion as a branch of jurisprudence strikes some observers as strange and even capricious. Judge A. B. Woodward, who corresponded with Jefferson and produced a serious treatise on classification, found much to praise in his friend's scheme but was dismayed that religion "comes out to be nothing more than *a part of jurisprudence*, and is the commencement of that branch, while commerce is the termination of it." He wondered if, "in strict language," either religion or commerce could be "parts of jurisprudence," particularly in a country that has taken the unprecedented step, led by Jefferson himself, of "disclaiming the right of interfering with religious sentiment." The judge's points are well taken, but Jefferson's unusual designation of religion as belonging to jurisprudence shows that he approached religion less as theology, for which he provided no category, and more as a sphere of institutionalized moral suasion. This is clarified somewhat in the modified scheme he created for his much smaller retirement library, where the Ethical branch of Philosophy is subdivided into Morality, Moral Supplements, and Social Organisation, and where Moral Supplements breaks down into two chapters, Religion and Law. Another innovation pointed out by Judge Woodward is Jefferson's treatment of Gardening, following Lord Kames's *Elements of Criticism*, as belonging to Fine Arts rather than Agriculture.[36]

As a practical instrument for everyday use, Jefferson's fully elaborated scheme was too cumbersome. In conferring upon James Ogilvie, his schoolmaster neighbor, the privilege of using the Monticello library while he was in Washington, Jefferson described in a letter his working arrangement: "1. Antient history. 2. Modern do. 3. Physics. 4. Nat. Hist. proper. 5. Technical arts. 6. Ethics. 7. Jurisprudence. 8. Mathematics. 9. Gardening, architecture, sculpture, painting, music, poetry. 10. Oratory 11. Criticism. 12. Polygraphical. You will find this on a paper nailed up somewhere in the library." The more usual arrangement of large libraries in Jefferson's day was alphabetical, but, as he explained to Watterston on 7 May 1815, he found this "very unsatisfactory, because of the medley it presents to the mind, the difficulty sometimes of recalling an author's name, and the greater difficulty, where the name is not given, of selecting the word in the title, which shall determine its alphabetical place. The arrangement according to subject is far preferable." The subject arrangement described to Ogilvie, with its emphasis on basic categories, would suffice for finding one's way around the library. The purpose of the catalog, on the other hand, was to function not so much as a finding aid as a detailed map showing where the contents of the books lay on the landscape of knowledge.[37]

By 1812, his manuscript catalog had become so congested with original entries, later additions, erasures, marginal insertions, and interlineations that Jefferson made a fair copy, in which he combined and reordered certain chapters, reducing their number from 46 to 44. Thus Politics and Commerce are combined into a single chapter, as are Gardening, Painting, and Sculpture. Some books he moved to a different chapter altogether, so that Ossian, once pronounced by Jefferson to be "the greatest Poet that has ever existed," is demoted from Epic to Romance. But the most important difference lay in the ordering of the books within the chapters. Far more deliberately than he had been able to do in the 1783 catalog, and with the entire collection before him, he gave the books of each chapter a meaningful catalog order that he described to Librarian of Congress Watterston, as "sometimes analytical, sometimes chronological, & sometimes a combination of both." This is the order that Watterston replaced, much to Jefferson's chagrin, with an alphabetical rendering in the catalog printed by Congress in 1815 and that E. Millicent Sowerby in her modern edition of the catalog sought to restore by recurrence to the order of the 1783 manuscript catalog, which, unlike the fair copy, still survives. But Jefferson substantially reorganized his catalog in the 1812 fair copy, as is demonstrated conclusively by the recent reappearance of a manuscript in the hand of Jefferson's grandson-in-law, Nicholas P. Trist, that proves to be a copy of the catalog of the library sold to Congress with the entries in Jefferson's order and corrected in his own hand. Here we see Jefferson's orderly and original mind at work, as he lays out his books on a variable grid that is "sometimes chronological," progressing from ancient to modern, "sometimes analytical," from general to particular, and "sometimes a combination of both," from theoretical to practical.[38]

"One of the most systematic of men," Dumas Malone wrote, "he was in character as a cataloguer." Jefferson's efforts to arrange and bring order to his library present the man in a representative action. Nothing that he would do would more perfectly capture his scholarly and exacting cast of mind, his distinctive intellectual combination of order and pragmatism. His strong sense of history is always present in the chronological aspect of the arrangement, which, even when it is not the overarching principle, is nonetheless a part of the pattern. Thus his chapter on architecture begins not with the treatises of his master Palladio, or even Palladio's model, Vitruvius, but with books on the ancient ruins. After a series of subtle transitions, in which the focus shifts from the ancient world to the modern and from period to place, he introduces the works of individual architects, the central arena of artistic theory and practice, and concludes his chapter with books needed by the practitioner, such as *Langley's practical Geometry* and *The Builder's Dictionary*. This deliberate ordering of historical, theoretical, and practical elements, which Jefferson characterized as "chronological" and "analytical," is more than an arrangement of disparate parts; it is, in fact, a carefully articulated whole.[39]

## THE RETIREMENT LIBRARY

In April 1815, the wagons that left Monticello for Washington carried the library that Thomas Jefferson had labored 45 years to create and which he believed to be, in a phrase that might sum up the grand plan, "the choicest collection of books in the United States." The rooms at the southern end of the first floor that had recently been filled to overflowing with 6,700 volumes were now quite empty, but Jefferson seems to have been neither sad nor regretful. In the first place, he was in serious financial straits and needed the $23,950 he received to meet pressing obligations. Nor was he entirely bereft of books, for he still had several hundred volumes of his favorite works in his petit format library at Poplar Forest. But the greatest consolation must have been the knowledge that his fondest wish for his library had been realized—that it would remain intact, just as he had built it, and preserved for the public weal as a permanent possession of the nation.[40]

"I cannot live without books," Jefferson wrote to John Adams on 10 June 1815, shortly after the wagons departed, "but fewer will suffice where amusement, and not use, is the only future object." In fact, he had already taken steps to acquire a good many replacements by this time, and Adams was to render valuable assistance by introducing him to George Ticknor, a precocious graduate of Dartmouth who was on his way to Europe. Jefferson was greatly impressed with Ticknor's learning and knowledge of books and quickly engaged him as a book-buying agent abroad. "Mr. Ticknor," he wrote Adams, "is particularly the best bibliograph I have met with, and very kindly and opportunely offered me the means of reprocuring some part of the literary treasures which I have ceded to Congress to replace the devastations of British Vandalism at Washington." It was through Ticknor that Jefferson first learned of and acquired, to his great delight, the superior editions of the classics produced by the notable German scholars of the period.[41]

On hearing that Jefferson's library was to go to Congress, Adams had written to his friend, "I envy you that immortal honour." These two former presidents, who had begun as political allies but whose friendship had been bitterly broken off, were happily reunited through the intercession of their mutual friend, Dr. Benjamin Rush. Their revived correspondence, which continued from 1812 until a few months before their deaths, is one of the ornaments of American letters. It began, appropriately enough, with an exchange of books. Adams sent Jefferson a copy of *Lectures on Rhetoric and Oratory* (1810) by his son, John Quincy Adams, and Jefferson responded with a copy of his own printed brief in the Batture case, *The Proceedings of the Government of the United States, in maintaining the Public Right to the Beach of the Missisipi, adjacent to New-Orleans, against the Intrusion of Edward Livingston* (1812). Both men were intensely bookish, and their letters abound with references to their reading. Even when they are cautiously feeling each other out in the initial stages of the correspondence, the touchstone is their reading. "I have given up newspapers," Jefferson writes somewhat disingenuously on 21 January 1812, " in exchange for Tacitus and Thucydides, for Newton and Euclid; and I find myself much the happier." Adams replies on 3 February with a pose of his own: "I have read Thucidides and Tacitus, so often, and at such distant Periods of my Life, that elegant, profound and enchanting as is their Style, I am weary of them. When I read them I seem to be only reading the History of my own Times and my own Life." As the correspondence progresses, the authors and titles of books fill their pages, as they discuss the Bible, Theocritus, translations of the Psalms, Endfield's *History of Philosophy*, Plato, Thomas Morton's *New English Canaan*, Theognis, and Joseph Priestley, to name only a few from the early letters. Their sparring over, they unburden themselves with a candor that is sometimes quite remarkable, as with Jefferson's unguarded dismissal of Plato's *Republic*: "While wading thro' the whimsies, the puerilities, and unintelligible jargon of this work, I laid it down often to ask myself how it could have been that the world should have so long consented to give reputation to such nonsense as this?"[42]

> Upon all thefe circumftances I am of opinion here is enoug
> ke it out of the common rule, and that this legacy is not to
> tisfaction of the debt.
>
> Vol. III.                                                    T. ˀ

*Jefferson's book mark. Typically, the only marks of ownership Jefferson wrote in his books were his own initials "T" and "I." These he placed unobtrusively on the pages containing the letters "I" and "T" (shown above) in the alphabetical succession of letters that indicated the order in which the printed gatherings of the book were to be bound.*

The libraries and reading tastes of the two old friends make for an interesting comparison. Adams' collection was not so large as Jefferson's, but his passion for books was at least as great. Argumentative by nature, Adams disputed with the authors in the margins of his books, where he was just as excitable and impatient as he was elsewhere. Jefferson, by contrast, rarely wrote anything in his books besides his special bookmark and an occasional cross-reference or correction. An exception is this wry annotation in a religious pamphlet: "doctrines not true prove the miracles not true. the miracles prove the doctrines & the doctrines prove the miracles, circularly." Adams's interests were also somewhat narrower than Jefferson's, having comparatively little in his library by way of belles lettres and far less in science and mathematics.[43]

In the 11 years that passed between the sale of his library and his death, Jefferson continued to acquire books at an astonishing rate, amassing a sizeable collection that would have had few peers. When the indebtedness of his estate required that his second Monticello library be put up for auction in 1829, the Washington bookseller, Nathaniel Poor, issued a catalog based on Jefferson's own, listing 931 titles and some 1,600 volumes. His retirement library would be for "amusement and not use," Jefferson had told Adams, meaning that he could dispense with much that had been necessary to support his public and private occupations and concentrate on books and subjects that engaged his deepest interests. The implied narrowing of scope is reflected in the catalog, which focuses on fewer writers and topics. Old favorites, such as the essays of Montaigne and Hume and Shaftesbury's *Characteristics*, are represented, and *Don Quixote*, said to be the only novel Jefferson ever reread, is present in two editions. A surprising amount of poetry is listed, though almost all of it from classical writers: Milton is there, but otherwise only a smattering of English poetry is included. The largest category, Jefferson's protests notwithstanding, is still politics, though much of it relates to recent American history and probably reflects not so much his intellectual interests as his obsession with the political events of his own time, which were often being called into dispute. In philosophy, as in other categories, the writers that drew his attention tend to be marked by the presence of several editions, so that nearly half of the 38 items listed under "Ethics—Antient" are devoted to only three writers: Epictetus, Cicero, and, surprisingly, Plato. Jefferson probably paid so much attention to this philosopher he so little admired (there were six entries relating to Plato) because of his impact on Christian theologians, a subject to which Jefferson often referred. Christianity was arguably a topic that engaged his interest as much as any other in his presidential and retirement years. Nearly one third of the 61 catalog entries under Religion are editions of or commentaries on the Bible, particularly the New Testament, and his letters to certain trusted correspondents show that he was deeply read in the development of Christianity from its founding to his own time.[44]

The most informative account of his retirement reading comes from his favorite granddaughter, Ellen Randolph Coolidge, who was her grandfather's secretary, companion, and student during these years:

> Books were at all times his chosen companions, and his acquaintance with many languages gave him great power of selection. He read Homer, Virgil, Dante, Corneille, Cervantes, as he read Shakspeare and Milton. In his youth he had loved poetry, but by the time I was old enough to observe, he had lost his taste for it, except for Homer and the great Athenian tragics, which he continued to the last to enjoy. He went over the works of Eschylus, Sophocles and Euripides, not very long before I left him [1825]. Of history he was very fond, and this he studied in all lan-

guages, though always, I think, preferring the ancients. In fact, he derived more pleasure from his acquaintance with Greek and Latin than from any other resource of literature, and I have often heard him express his gratitude to his father for causing him to receive a classical education. I saw him more frequently with a volume of the classics in his hand than with any other book.

Though he sold his great library to Congress, Jefferson never lacked for books, and his frequent protests about the lack of time for reading need to be understood in the context of his wishes rather than in absolute terms, for the amount of reading he succeeded in doing was prodigious by any standard. Plagued as he was in his retirement by a multitude of unwelcome distractions, as well as financial and family difficulties, he responded by indulging what he himself described as "a canine appetite for reading."[45]

## THE LIBRARY AND THE LEGACY

Thomas Jefferson was a man for whom books were "a necessary of life." They were the indispensable tools of his work, whether the law, government, or farming, and they were his favorite recreation. The case of Patrick Henry, who had comparatively little use for books and reading, mystified him, and he wondered where Henry's golden eloquence could have come from. His own talents and abilities had been carefully cultivated from his earliest days, and he spared no effort of research to extend or enhance his knowledge. The Marquis de Chastellux, when he visited Monticello in April 1782, remarked on his host's impressive "mind and attainments" and described him for his European readers as "an American, who, *without ever having quitted his own country*, is Musician, Draftsman, Surveyor, Astronomer, Natural Philosopher, Jurist, and Statesman." The attainments that so impressed the sophisticated Frenchman, in a man who lived in the middle of nowhere and had never traveled abroad, were mostly earned or prepared for in his library.[46]

Being recognized as an extraordinarily learned man was part of Jefferson's public character from the outset of his career. Before they were well acquainted, John Adams was attracted to him because he had been described by a friend as "the greatest rubber off of dust" he had ever known. Jefferson was constantly being consulted on matters relating to books and education and conscientiously made out dozens of reading lists at the requests of his friends. Not surprisingly, this reputation had its negative side as well. One of the things always said about him by his critics and political enemies was that he was an impractical theorist, the captive of mere book learning. Even those who conceded his greatness could not resist this means of neutralizing his opinions, as in the case of Matthew Carey, who genuinely admired him but whose zealous promotion of native manufacturing seemed to require a denunciation of Jefferson's agrarianism, outlined so memorably in the *Notes on Virginia*. "His Arcadia," Carey wrote, "must have been sought, not in Virginia or Maryland, but in Virgil's or Pope's pastorals, or Thomson's seasons." Unfair as this is to Jefferson's much-altered views on manufacturing subsequent to the *Notes*, there is a measure of truth in the charge that his vision of a society made up of "those who labor in the earth" owed much to his reading. Great learning has its vulnerabilities, and Jefferson was apparently content to accept them. As Merrill D. Peterson has written, "Emerson's idea that the reading of books warped or suffocated the scholar would have been incomprehensible to Jefferson."[47]

Eventually, reading and study came to represent more than an occupational means and a recreational end. He had long believed that the state should provide public schools and libraries to insure an enlightened citizenry and thus preserve democracy. As he grew older and became more engrossed in the struggle for mutual toleration and rational self-government, he began to speak of learning as a political and even a moral responsibility. "Enlighten the people generally," he advised his friend P. S. Dupont de Nemours, "and tyrany and oppressions of body and mind will vanish like evil spirits at the dawn of day." This remark bears not only on the benefits that will accrue to the people but on the responsibilities of the learned. Near the end of his life he wrote that "The cultivation of science [i. e. knowledge] is an act of religious duty to the Author of our being." By a similar progression, his early plan for a comprehensive library came eventually to have, as with so many Jeffersonian endeavors, an important public dimmension, and at some point he determined that his collection should not remain "private property."[48]

The need for a replacement for the congressional library in 1814 was thus a timely opportunity for Thomas Jefferson to place his splendid collection at the disposal of the public. The second Monticello library, as we have seen, was sold at auction three years after his death. These books are now in public and private libraries, including the Library of Congress, which purchased some items at the dispersal sale and has added others since. The Poplar Forest library, containing the petit format collection, remained the property of Jefferson's grandson, Francis Eppes, until 1873, when it was advertised to be sold at auction. A number of these volumes have found their way to another library originally chosen by Thomas Jefferson, that of the University of Virginia, which has, for example, his set of Bell's petit format edition of the English Poets.[49]

The 6,700 books that went to Washington in 1815 became the nucleus of the Library of Congress, and as such were subjected to the rigors of regular use. Some were lent out and lost, while others were repaired or rebound in such a way as to obliterate their provenance. But most devastating was a fire in the Capitol on Christmas Eve in 1851 that destroyed nearly two thirds of the original Jefferson volumes. Not until the twentieth century were the surviving books assembled and set apart as a special collection within the Library. When E. Millicent Sowerby was retained in the 1940s to compile a catalog of the books Jefferson had sold to Congress, she was able to identify some additional books still in the stacks as having been part of the original purchase. Her *Catalogue of the Library of Thomas Jefferson* (1952-1959), an invaluable work in five large volumes, contains bibliographical information on the works known or believed to be in Jefferson's library when it came to Congress, as well as extracts on books and authors from his letters and other writings. An unfortunate limitation of this catalog is that, in being restricted to the great library, it does not include the multitude of volumes in the retirement library (the second Monticello and the Poplar Forest collection), nor does it take into account the many other books otherwise known to have been in his possession.

Of all the treasures in the Library of Congress, perhaps none is more highly prized than the 2,465 surviving volumes from the library of Thomas Jefferson. They are kept together under controlled atmospheric conditions in the Rare Book and Special Collections Division, where they are frequently called for and examined by scholars. Many have been rebound and bear the marks of prolonged use, though others are still in their original bindings and are in excellent condition. A few sections have survived in surprising completeness, such as the those on religion and law, while others, such as the chapters on literature, are almost entirely absent. Some volumes still display the bookplate or signature of distinguished previous owners: William Byrd II, Peyton Randolph, Richard Bland, and George Wythe. A few have "Ex Libris Thomæ Jefferson" inscribed in his hand on the title page, which seems to represent an early practice, but most carry only the tiny, unobtrusive initials that Jefferson settled on as his private book mark.

In one sense, it might be said that Jefferson's library is now only a cherished remnant, a priceless portion of a once-great collection. But it seems truer to say that during the nearly two centuries it has belonged to the nation, Jefferson's library has grown prodigiously in size and in stature until it has become a great national library, one of the finest and most accessible in the world. Just as its richly ornamented main building on Capitol Hill now bears his name, so the Library of Congress, in collecting and preserving materials on every subject from every part of the world for the use and benefit of all, faithfully perpetuates the spirit and ideals of Thomas Jefferson.